THE
MENSA
GENIUS
A·B·C
QUIZ BOOK

THE MENSA GENIUS

A·B·C QUIZ BOOK

ALAN STILLSON

and the members of American Mensa, Ltd.

PERSEUS BOOKS

Reading, Massachusetts

Many of the designations used by manufacturers and sellers to distinguish their products are claimed as trademarks. Where those designations appear in this book and Perseus Books was aware of a trademark claim, the designations have been printed in initial capital letters (e.g., Dirt Devil).

Mensa is a registered trademark and service mark of American Mensa, Ltd. It is used in this book with the permission of American Mensa, Ltd.

Library of Congress Cataloging-in-Publication Data

Stillson, Alan.
    The Mensa genius A-B-C quiz book / Alan Stillson and the members of American Mensa, Ltd.
      p. cm.
    ISBN 0-201-31135-6
    1. Word games. 2. Puzzles.   I. American Mensa Limited.
II. Title.
GV1507.W8S76   1998
793.73—dc21   98-13906
                                        CIP

Perseus Books is a member of the Perseus Books Group

Cover design by Suzanne Heiser
Text design by Karen Savary
Set in 12-point Minion by Karen Savary Studio

2 3 4 5 6 7 8 9–DOH–0201009998
Second printing, June 1998

Find us on the World Wide Web at
http://www.aw.com/gb/

Perseus Books are available at special discounts for bulk purchases in the U.S. by corporations, institutions, and other organizations. For more information, please contact the Special Markets Department at HarperCollins Publishers, 10 East 53rd Street, New York, NY 10022, or call 212-207-7528.

To Gail and our ever-supportive extended family, including Jeff, Debi, Howard, Cedelle, Jill, Gary, Jack, Rose, Sharon, Steven, Helene, Jocelyn, Dave, and Sam

Contents

Foreword

Little did the late Marvin Grosswirth and I know what we started when we created the first *Mensa Genius Quiz Book.* The "Match Wits with Mensa" feature fascinated hundreds of thousands of readers, and the book, first published in 1981, is still selling. Another two books followed, and now there is a fourth in the line of "Match Wits with Mensa." Hooray!

Alan Stillson, a member of Mensa and a wonderful puzzle expert, has written a book, similar in concept, but with entirely new puzzles, including several types of verbal puzzles never seen before (at least by me). He has matched Mensa members against his skill.

Mr. Stillson has also continued the tradition and original purpose of the Mensa books. A substantial portion of the royalties from this series goes toward

Mensa scholarships. Mensa scholarships were started in the early 1970s under the direction of Marvin Grosswirth, the organization's chairman at the time. They are unique. They are based, in general, not on financial need, nor academic achievement, nor I.Q. scores. They are based on commitment. Mensa commits its money; the applicants must commit themselves. Applicants at any level from college freshmen to postdoctoral students, working for a degree in an American-accredited institution of higher learning, submit a 550-word essay, which is judged anonymously. This essay must contain a statement of the applicant's life's goals and *what the applicant has done to achieve them.* A student who wants to be a doctor, cure cancer, and save lives won't get an award, but an applicant who has been a candy striper for five years, worked in a medical lab during school vacations, and done a small amount of research with the family doctor will score very high on the rating scale. That applicant has demonstrated a dedication and a purpose and has worked to achieve it. Part of the proceeds of Mr. Stillson's book will help to reward these serious, dedicated scholars.

Now a brief bit about Mensa, for those readers who are encountering this unique society for the first time. *Mensa,* which means "table" in Latin, was founded by Dr. L. L. Ware and the late Roland Berrill when they were at Oxford after World War II. It was originally thought of as a roundtable of equals, for serious intellectual discussions. Of course, the organization being what it is, the official logo is a SQUARE table. That's Mensa for you.

The society grew slowly in Great Britain. Roland Berrill died young, and for a long time, Mensa remained a purely British organization. Then, in 1960, Victor Serebriakoff, a bouncing, energetic go-getter, full of ideas, arrived in New York to start an American chapter. He eventually hired the late Margot Seitelman as executive director, and the American baby soon outgrew its parent. Mensa International also took off, and now there are several dozen recognized Mensas around the world, in Canada, France, Germany, Malaysia, Australia and New Zealand, and many other nations, and even more emerging Mensas, as they are called, in countries that were formerly in closed territory, such as Hungary, Slovakia, the Czech Republic, and more, some of which will be full-fledged operating Mensas by the time this book is published.

In short, the appeal of Mensa crosses all national boundaries, all ethnic and religious lines, and all geographical barriers. The idea is appealing—a worldwide society of equals, held together solely by the glue of intelligence and friendship—with no political agenda, no opinions, and no barriers. Mensa is one of the most democratic societies in the world. It has only one requirement: a score on a standardized, supervised intelligence test (or the equivalent) at or above the 98th percentile. In the United States that translates to a score of 132 on the Stanford-Binet and most school tests, 130 on the various Wechsler Intelligence Scales, and 148 on the Raven's Advanced Progressive Matrices. Mensa does much of its own testing, and, of course, has tests available that have been normed for other than a standard American, English-speaking population.

And just what does Mensa do? I can speak from experience here, having been a member for considerably more than thirty years. It has local chapters that run everything from dinner meetings, to great books discussions, to poker games, to what are called Regional Gatherings (a term taken from the British), where members of several local groups, and often from far away, join for several days of lectures, games, and above all, social interaction. The Annual Gathering can draw up to 1,500 members (and guests) from around the world. It is three or four days of interesting, amusing, informative lectures, games rooms, contests, and awards banquets for the volunteers who run Mensa, which has a paid staff of only a dozen. The volunteers are what makes Mensa so fascinating. They tend to have their own ideas and, being volunteers, feel free to express them. Many of our best and most interesting events have come about because volunteers were willing to work to put on an event they thought would be interesting.

A significant attraction in Mensa is its Special Interest Groups. These range from quilting to wine-making, and everything in between. As a Mensa member, if you don't find a Special Interest Group that matches your special interest, you can go out and start one, subject to the rules governing such groups. The

Special Interest Groups operate basically by mail, publish newsletters, and provide a part of the colorful fabric that makes up the Mensa patchwork.

Finally, there is the Mensa Education and Research Foundation. This separate 501(c)3 entity, known as MERF, awards the scholarships. It also sponsors research grants, gifted-children projects, and other educational and charitable activities, in accordance with its charter, which basically states that it should help to foster intelligence.

In short, whatever you are looking for, if you qualify for Mensa, you'll probably find it somewhere under the Mensa umbrella. With members ranging from truck drivers to nuclear engineers, look and you will find.

Marvin and I had fun writing the first and second books. I had fun doing the third. Readers apparently had fun reading them and matching their wits against those of the Mensas who participated. Now you have a chance to join the group of happy puzzle solvers, match your wits against those of the top 2 percent, and—who knows?—perhaps even decide to join the group.

Happy puzzle solving!

—*Abbie F. Salny*

Introduction

Bach, Mozart, and Beethoven are to music
as
Carroll, Dudeney, and Loyd are to...?

The answer is "puzzles." Lewis Carroll, Henry Dudeney, and Sam Loyd drew on an art form that had been around for centuries and refined it, creating masterpieces that we recognize as both modern and timeless. They were prolific puzzle makers, and they inspired all of us who followed.

Lewis Carroll, whose real name was Charles Dodgson, was an English mathematics professor who lived from 1832 to 1898. He wrote thousands of original puzzles in and beyond his classic children's books,

Alice in Wonderland and *Through the Looking-Glass.* Carroll specialized in logic problems, wordplay, and a form he called doublets, which ask us to form a chain from one word to another, changing one letter at a time. Henry Dudeney, another English giant in this field, lived from 1857 to 1930. He wrote *Amusements in Mathematics* and published a wide assortment of mathematics puzzles, chess problems, and word games. Sam Loyd, an American who lived from 1841 to 1911, compiled his many brainteasers into *Sam Loyd's Cyclopedia of 5,000 Puzzles, Tricks and Conundrums.*

One trait that united these modern puzzle masters was their love of language, in all its forms. But all humans love language games to some extent. Wordplay has been around nearly as long as words have. For centuries Japanese poets have composed haiku, a term formed from two Chinese characters that mean "playful phrases." When Julius Caesar reportedly said of Gaul, *"Veni, vidi, vici,"* he was playing on the alliteration of "I came, I saw, I conquered" in Latin. Even the ancient riddle of the Sphinx—"What walks on four feet in the morning, two feet at noon, and three feet in the evening?"—requires us to consider what words can mean metaphorically. Carroll, Dudeney, and Loyd had millennia of wordplay to build on.

That tradition has continued to develop. The twentieth century has seen the invention of the crossword puzzle (designed in quite different forms around the world). In the 1950s and 1960s, more notable creators emerged. Martin Gardner wrote many puzzle books as well as a long-running monthly column for *Scientific American*. Publisher and game-show panelist Bennett Cerf wrote numerous books on riddles and wordplay. Before he became famous for popularizing jogging, Mensa member Jim Fixx wrote *Games for the Superintelligent*. Today such authors as Paul Sloan (*Lateral Thinking*), Helen Nash (*Cryptograms*), Will Shortz (crossword puzzle editor of the *New York Times* and former editor of *Games* magazine), and Abbie Salny (American Mensa's Supervisory Psychologist) carry on this long tradition.

Why have we humans always asked riddles, worked out puns, and wracked our brains over questions we knew would turn out to be tricks? The clinical psychiatrist's answer may be complicated, but the puzzle lover's answer is simple: they're fun.

What a great feeling it is to figure out a riddle, to spot a pun, to find the eight letters that spell out "a large water-loving rodent" (capybara)! Whatever form the puzzles take, the joy of working on them is the joy of figuring something out. And it's especially fun to figure out something about words, those little collections of symbols or sounds that we depend on every day.

In today's busy world, the potential pleasure of solving a time-consuming puzzle is often lost to other demands. That's why this book is designed so that you can enjoy one puzzle at a time, or as many as you want to do. Most of the word games in this book can be completed in less than a minute—either you'll figure one out or you'll figure out that you won't figure it out without some library work. Only a few require writing anything down. Yes, it's possible to experience the joy of puzzles when you want and in as little or as much time as you choose.

When you're ready to look at the answer to a particular puzzle, look for the dark patch on the outside of the page. Match that patch to the corresponding dark patch in the Solutions (riffle the side of the book if you have to). The numbers on the sides of the pages will guide you to the correct answer. Try not to peek at the others!

For further pleasure, this book also gives you an opportunity to "Match Wits with Mensa." Each of these puzzles has been tested by a panel of brave volunteers from American Mensa, Ltd., as the next section explains in detail.

Just as some words have two meanings, some of these puzzles have two or more valid answers, listed in the Solutions. Give yourself full credit if you come up with any of them. When two or more members of the Mensa testing panel suggested the same wrong answer, I mentioned it in the Solutions as well—under "not"! You may not be able to give yourself credit for those answers, but at least you can tell yourself that you're thinking like a Mensa member.

Finally, it's quite possible that you might discover an alternative answer not mentioned in the Solutions. Check your sources to be sure you're right. Then give yourself extra credit!

This is a puzzle book, not a scientific test. If you

want to track your results against the testing panel, go ahead. If you don't want to, don't. Puzzle books are for fun. Doing well doesn't guarantee success in anything else, and doing not so well (whatever that means to you) is no sure sign of trouble where "gray matter" matters. The one conclusion that you can draw is that it takes a hefty combination of word power, imagination, and general knowledge to score at least 55 percent in this puzzle book.

Stumped? Remember that words have many facets. They have shapes, sounds, grammar, meanings, histories, contexts, and ingredients. Here are fifteen hints of where to probe for a breakthrough:

1. Look for words or expressions with more than one meaning.

2. Count letters, syllables, and so on.

3. Consider pronunciation and sounds.

4. Check alphabetical order.

5. Play with letters: reverse them, add new ones, delete some.

6. Look for words within words.

7. Spot common or unusual letter combinations.

8. Consider key words and phrases.

9. Review parts of speech.

10. Notice uncommon sentence structure and grammar.

11. Beware of simplicity disguised as complexity.

12. Don't forget common names, brand names, abbreviations, and colloquialisms.

13. Review your knowledge of popular culture, sports, and hobbies.

14. Consider your practical, academic, and artistic knowledge.

15. Finally, remember that puzzle-makers enjoy sharing imaginative uses of words and phrases.

The "Match Wits with Mensa" Panel

All of the puzzles in this book were tested by 104 Mensa members selected on the basis of just one quality—their willingness to participate. The panel included students, professors, doctors, lawyers, and retirees. Members' ages ranged from the teens to over seventy. Some testers had published puzzles in magazines, others had served on the testing panels for previous books in this series, and for some English was a second language.

To the panel members I mailed all the puzzles in this book (and a few more). They responded within two weeks, answering as many puzzles as they could in that time. I then calculated the percentage of testers who answered each question correctly, rounding off to the nearest 5 percent. That figure appears in parentheses with the answer to each puzzle. A small percentage—as low as 5 percent—indicates that the puzzle was especially difficult even for Mensa volunteers.

For each section of the book, you'll see the average score of the Mensa testing panel on that set of puzzles. Naturally, that score varies depending on the difficulty of the puzzles and the amount of general knowledge they test. Overall, the Mensa volunteers answered an average of 55 percent of the puzzles in this book correctly. So let that percentage be your benchmark as you "Match Wits with Mensa"!

My first round of thanks goes to the leaders of the Greater Los Angeles Mensa writers' group for inspiration and valuable critiques: Marty Elkort, Jerry Hicks, and Sonny Cooper.

The next round of thanks goes to members of Greater Los Angeles Mensa for preliminary puzzle testing and initial editing: Roy Ball, Jana Bickell, Rhonda Byer, Andy Cohen, Flo Cohen, Joy Gaylord, Barbara Harvey, Victor Huang, Gloria Krauss, Stratton Lindemeyer, Mirk Mirkin, Kathryn Morrison, Ken Rosenchek, and Betty Schneider.

And the last round of thanks goes to 104 additional members of American Mensa for puzzle testing and further editing: Marion Alpern (IN), Damon Antos (FL), Daniel Babcock (MO), Rod Baker (CA),

Stephen H. Bauer (OR), Wendy Bell (TN), Nancy
Beringer (NH), Ginni Betts (IL), John H. Bickford
(MA), George Blance (MA), David Broome (AZ), Lois
Cappellano (MA), Paul Conover (PA), Kimberly A.
Cope (MN), Lois Corsello (CA), Karen Darmetko (FL),
Maryann Donovan (CA), Nancy Eisenmann (CT), Ted
Elzinga (CA), Mary Ensley (AL), Dara Esfandiary
(DC), Thomas L. Fagan (PA), Bill Fisher (IN), Rita
Foudray (TX), Peter Fuchs (NC), Thomas G. Funk
(AL), Barney Gallussio (NJ), Bonita M. Garvey (FL),
Esther Gottlieb (NY), David N. Groff (PA), Thomas
Gunning III (TX), Kent B. Hake (IL), Charles Hall
(IN), Monroe Harden (KY), Megan Heber (OH), John
T. Henderson (FL), Maynard J. Hirshon (FL), Amy
Holm (AZ), Emily Hsuan (CA), Jane Hsuan (CA), Karl
Kabanek (TX), David P. Keeser (WA), Charles Keifer
(MA), Amy Kent (PA), Steve Krattiger (CA), Linda
Kriegel (NJ), Carol Kuhns (OH), Nancy Laine (OH),
Larry Larson (OR), Steve Latterell (IL), Richard A.
LeCain (NH), David Leith (TX), David Linko (PA),
Richard Loeffler (WI), Susan Macke (KS), Michael W.
Maher (MI), Jennifer Martin (CA), Celia Manolesco
(CA), Douglas G. May (WA), Mike Mayer (OH),
Palmer McCurdy (VA), Alan T. McDonald (VA), John
Mochan (FL), James J. Murphy (NY), Kevin Murray
(FL), Sastry Nanduri (NJ), Sandra J. Nelson (IA), Dawn
Novak (AR), Shane J. Orr (IA), Chuck Osborne (IL),
Shawn Otto (MN), Tony Parillo (CA), G. Vaughan
Parker (CA), Jeffrey L. Peace (OH), Rena Popna (NH),
Thomas W. Reeves (TX), David F. Ries (MA), Bob

Roach (MN), Elizabeth Roberts (WA), Guy Rosenschein (NY), Brad Sanford (TN), Rorianne Schrade (NY), Larry Schwartz (CT), Lisa Schwartz (VA), Harold C. Sebring (VA), Jim Segerson (WI), Jason Sharpe (TX), Wm. Sheehan (MA), Scott Sheldon (NJ), Joseph A. Spadero (CT), Gene Staver (WI), David Steinberg (VA), Steve Story (FL), John Suarez (CA), Steve Swiader (RI), Greg Taylor (OH), Richard Till (IA), Heidi Van Ert (UT), Deborah Vernier (NV), Paul Westley (UK), Chuck Wiese (IA), Jefferson Wolski (TN), Rachel Young (MI), and Matt Zimmermann (KS).

chapter 1

No-Pencil Quickies

LIMERICKS

For those who like puzzles in verse, a limerick may be too terse. Just five lines of clues yield few answers to choose from; only a haiku is worse. Here's one example of a limerick puzzle:

> Penning works that were fit for a king,
> I created the world's longest ring.
> You will need at least four
> Lengthy evenings or more
> If you want to take in the whole thing.

The answer is "Richard Wagner," the composer of *The Ring of the Nibelung,* a cycle of four full-length operas (literally "works").

The answers to the following puzzles can be people, things, places, words, or abstract nouns. Can you name the subject of each of the following limericks?

(The average score of the Mensa testing panel on these poetic puzzles was 65 percent.)

1

I'm amazing 'cause I've got the force
To hold down a cow or a horse.
As you've doubtlessly found,
I am always around,
And I'm constantly working, of course.

2

I knew who I was long ago,
Though no one today seems to know.
Every year, millions cry
At the grave where I lie,
In the sunshine, the rain, and the snow.

3

On the charts, I remain number one;
This position cannot be undone.
If I burn, you may get
Just a little bit wet.
In a zeppelin, I am no fun.

4

Though in theory I'm always behind you,
I'm also around to remind you.
But in case it's your way
To give me too much say,
I can hamper or, even worse, blind you.

5

I'm a unit of heat generation.
I am prone to great quantification.
There are many aware
Of the numbers I bear—
Some in triumph, and some in frustration.

6

A metropolis in the U.S.,
I hold millions of people, no less.
But if you were to be
Just a mile south of me,
Would that put you in Canada? Yes!

7

I am just a small letter, you see,
As irrational as I can be.
Though it sounds quite insane,
When I'm cubed, you'll obtain
The negative of little me.

8

As a worker, I'm earning my pay.
When I hear what the first people say,
Then I change every word
So the things that are heard
By the others can help make their day.

9

There are times I'm a spot or a grade
Or a strike or a spare that was made;
I have also gained fame
As a masculine name
And a person on whom tricks are played.

FLOWERY MOVIE TITLES

Sometimes people with large vocabularies use unnecessarily flowery language. Sometimes even Mensa members do! For example, the title of not one but two Alfred Hitchcock thrillers could have been "The Male Homo Sapiens with an Overabundance of Accumulated Data." Fortunately, the title he used for both versions of this classic was *The Man Who Knew Too Much.*

What were the original names behind the following florid movie titles?

(The "Match Wits with Mensa" panel scored an average of 65 percent on these puzzles.)

1
GREETINGS, HANDTRUCK

2
TAURUS THROWING A TANTRUM

3
OCCIDENTALLY LOCATED NARRATIVE

4
THE GARGANTUAN FACILE

5
SOLAR SATELLITE OF THE MEMBERS OF THE PONGIDAE FAMILY

6
DISTANCE DIVIDED BY TIME

7
OBLITERATED FROM EXISTENCE IN CONJUNCTION WITH ATMOSPHERIC VAPORS IN MOTION

8
DEPARTING FROM THE MOST POPULOUS METROPOLITAN AREA OF THE SILVER STATE

STRANGE QUESTIONS

Here's a classic puzzle that ends with an unexpected question:

> A bear walks ten miles due south, ten miles east, and ten miles north, ending up on the spot where it started. What color was the bear?

The answer is white. And the reason is that there are very few places on the globe where one can take that walk and end up in the same place—all of them on or near the North Pole or near the South Pole. Since there are no bears on Antarctica, and the only bears in the Arctic are polar bears, this bear has to be white.

Here are some new puzzles with equally strange questions at the ends.

(The Mensa testers answered 55 percent of these puzzles correctly on average.)

1 The Missing Cards

Eight cards were missing from a standard poker deck with no jokers, making it impossible to get a straight flush. Which cards were missing?

2 The Basketball Team

Avery, Jones, Robinson, Kucic, and Himmel-farb are the starting players on the college basketball team. Avery, who wears jersey number 30, told number 45, Jones, that Robinson was the mean one. Kucic, who wears number 35, told Himmelfarb that Avery was absolutely right. But Robinson, number 40, is even-tempered and kind to everybody. What number is on Himmel-farb's jersey?

3 The Emergency Call

Halfway through the season, Kucic the bas-ketball player was hurried into the largest hospital in Lexington, Kentucky. The admit-ting nurse called Dr. Masterson's emergency beeper. In five minutes Dr. Masterson called back. The nurse explained the emergency and asked, "Where are you?"

"We're in the middle of Gary, Indiana," she heard the doctor say.

"How long will it take you to get here?"

"Two minutes."

What was Dr. Masterson doing when she received the emergency call?

4 The Cause of Hospitalization

Kucic's mother received a call from the college basketball coach. "I'm sorry, Mrs. Kucic," the coach said, "but during our Kentucky game your son had to be taken to the hospital. Don't worry, I understand it's the largest—"

"What's wrong?" Mrs. Kucic wailed.

The coach's reply echoed in her mind: "I'm afraid the booze got to him…. I'm afraid the booze got to him." Mrs. Kucic was too shocked to hear anything else. Her son had never drunk alcohol before going to college. And the coach had assured her that the campus had strict rules against underage drinking.

In fact, Kucic was not drunk and was not injured. What had caused his hospitalization?

5 The Violin Lesson

During Santiago's violin lesson, Professor Arion suddenly said, "You really should play piano."

Santiago kept on playing the violin.

Finally, Professor Arion clapped his hands and said, "Good!"

What change had Santiago made in his violin playing?

6 The Football Game

Andy and Mike, who live in the bay area, had a busy Sunday. They drove 20 miles west and went to the 49ers game in the afternoon. Then they drove about 120 miles nearly due east to their favorite seafood restaurant and had dinner overlooking the ocean. Whom did the 49ers play?

7 The Jumpy Pilot

The airline pilot Captain King has stopped going to the employees' lounge at the airport. Whenever he entered, his colleagues would call out informal greetings, naturally upsetting everyone else in the room. It didn't matter whether they called to him with just his first name or his full name—he was still causing too many scares. What is Captain King's first name?

8 The Transfer Student

After Elspeth Peters's family moved from Leeds to Phoenix, she had to take a placement exam for her new high school. Her best subject, she knew, was chemistry. And, indeed, her science teacher congratulated her on scoring 99 percent.

"How can that be?" Elspeth asked. "The test asked me to identify elements from their chemical symbols. There were only ten questions!"

"And you did very well," said the science teacher, "but I had to take off one point for spelling."

What element had tripped up this exemplary chemistry student?

9 The Active Activist

After two years, Tom Antonucci was stepping down from being the secretary of a group of animal rights activists. To show him a good time, some of the members took him out one sunny day. Tom shot an eagle, and everyone congratulated him. Where had they gone?

10 The Repeat Customer

John Travis was a man of habits, even when he was traveling. From January to December 1997, no matter what American city he was in, he made the same $3.84 purchase with a $5.00 bill and received back the same four coins. What did he buy?

ABBREVIATIONS

Every field must have its own abbreviations. For instance, Mensa is full of SIGs (Special Interest Groups). On the back of this book you'll find its ISBN (International Standard Book Number).

Abbreviations can become complicated when several are used together. For example, a trucker going from Los Angeles to Phoenix, Tucson, El Paso, and San Antonio might note her route as LA/PHX/TUC/EP/SA. A baseball coach might use P, C, 1B, 2B, 3B, SS, LF, CF, RF for the fielding positions of pitcher, catcher, first base, second base, third base, shortstop, left field, center field, and right field.

What do the following lists of abbreviations mean?

(The "Match Wits with Mensa" panel scored 65 percent on this section. Like them, for your answer you can identify most of the abbreviated items, state the underlying reasoning, or both.)

1
ARI, ALG, GEO, TRI, PRO, STA, CAL

2
COM, DRA, ADV, ACT, SPO, MUS, HOR, SCI

3
VLN, VLA, CEL, BA, TRU, TRO, FH

4
SON, SAM, MIT, GOL, TOS, PAN, ZEN, QUA

5
CEL, KNI, BUL, ROC, CAV, JAZ, LAK

6
LGA, LAX, SFO, DAL, SEA, MIA, DET

7
YOS, YEL, OLY, GLA, CAR, MAM, EVE, SHE

8
FIR, GDY, DUN, GDR, MIC, KEL, UNI

FLOWERY SONG TITLES

In theory, flowery language is just right for songs. When Fats Waller sang, "Your pedal extremities are colossal," didn't that sound better than that song's synonymous title: "Your Feet's Too Big"? Unfortunately, extraneous verbiage can be burdensome to articulate. Try crooning "Planet Satellite Riparian Entity" instead of "Moon River."

What were the original names of the following flowery song titles? (Hint: each came from, or is strongly associated with, a movie.)

(The Mensa puzzle testers correctly transposed 65 percent of these songs.)

1

Individual components of liquid precipitation are relentlessly descending upon this individual's cranium

2

Elevated aspirations

3

The moment within the continuum of time in which you relate a personal desire to the center of a group of planets

4

Coincident with the passage of the ratio of distance to velocity

5

A 1,440-minute interval exists in which my monarch's male offspring will arrive

6

Exhale with an audible sound of controllable pitch in the process of performing labor

7

Above the natural spectrum following liquid precipitation

8

Permit us to exit to aviate a quadrilateral all of whose sides are equal to one adjacent side and unequal to another and with perpendicular diagonals

9

Homo sapiens preceded with commercially acceptable mixtures typically consisting of sucrose, pectin, and numerous combinations of edible stimulants

10

The universal set of humans is verbalizing

THREEESQUES

As of this writing, there are no English words in the dictionary containing consecutive triple letters. But we could make up some. If an ornament using classical Arabic motifs is an "arabesque," then a word using a triple motif could be a "threeesque." If something easy to loathe is "loathsome," something easy to iron could be "presssome." And what would a male calf be? If a baby pig is a "piglet," a baby bull would be a "bulllet." Who knows? One day these threeesques might be in the dictionary.

Using similar reasoning and lots of imagination, what words with consecutive triple letters could you make up to fit the following definitions?

(Members of the Mensa testing panel averaged 55 percent on these threeesques. But between them they found at least two new words for every definition below. For full credit, all you have to find is one.)

1

THE OWNER OF A PASSAGEWAY IN A BUILDING

2

A CHART OF CHICKEN PRODUCTIVITY

3

A FAIRY-TALE EXPERT

4

A SERIOUS CLIMBER OF LOW HILLS

5

THE STUDY OF THE LARGEST MARSUPIALS

6

A PLACE TO MAKE MISTAKES

7

THE LONGEVITY OF A LIGHT BULB

8

AN ECCENTRIC GAUGE

chapter
2

Commoner Puzzles

Commoner puzzles are made up of two columns with five things (words, names, and places) in each. The goal is to find what all the things in Column A have in common that none of the things in Column B shares as well. Here are two examples:

COLUMN A	COLUMN B
Allegiance	Practical
Flag	Yard
Of	Drum
Republic	Patriotic
Stand	Sit

Solution: All the words in Column A are in the "Pledge of Allegiance."

COLUMN A	COLUMN B
Hammer	Porter
Soothe	Hardly
Spleen	Kidney
Attend	Cleric
Stress	Murmur

Solution: All the words in Column A have a consecutive double letter.

MISCELLANY

(The Mensa panel solved 45 percent of these commoner puzzles on average.)

1

COLUMN A	COLUMN B
Mud	Flour
Lemonade	Glass
Cement	Steel
Tea	Onyx
Coffee	Oxygen

2

COLUMN A	COLUMN B
Lime	Pear
Apple	Plum
Pineapple	Lemon
Cantaloupe	Honeydew
Orange	Fig

3

COLUMN A	COLUMN B
Lung	Pillow
Cast	Drip
Horse	Oat
Maiden	Jump
Grid	Loud

4

COLUMN A	COLUMN B
Birds	Salesmen
Rings	Lions
Lords	Carpenters
Maids	Skunks
Hens	Surfers

5

COLUMN A	COLUMN B
Bear	Lion
Grouse	Alligator
Carp	Moth
Fly	Dolphin
Duck	Cougar

6

COLUMN A	COLUMN B
Mercury	Aluminum
Gold	Magnesium
Iron	Phosphorus
Potassium	Sulphur
Lead	Chromium

7

COLUMN A	COLUMN B
Friend	Club
Hard	Barn
Owner	Please
Steam	Circle
Court	Enough

8

COLUMN A	COLUMN B
Dialogue	Borderline
Education	Oxygen
Facetious	Biological
Outpatient	Questionable
Regulation	Chop

9

COLUMN A	COLUMN B
Gifts	Plane
Down	Oak
Resemblance	Sure
Pain	Shy
Grudge	Blue

10

COLUMN A	COLUMN B
Kangaroo	Deer
Chimpanzee	Orangutan
Boa	Crocodile
Flea	Elephant
Caribou	Flamingo

11

COLUMN A	COLUMN B
Junk	Peck
Blank	Speak
Cask	Flank
Sock	Work
Mark	Truck

12

COLUMN A	COLUMN B
Fig	Crane
Case	Sprig
Ease	Oar
Pig	Vase
Base	Blind

13

COLUMN A	COLUMN B
Unique	Placid
Piccolo	Chart
Shock	Indict
Kindle	Moderate
Because	Cipher

14

COLUMN A	COLUMN B
Astronomical	Lack
Raze	Portable
Ape	Rocket
Loom	Usual
Listening	Atom

15

COLUMN A	COLUMN B
Facts	Trump
Boiled	Read
Ware	Yard
Knocks	And
Pressed	Breadth

SAME-SIZE WORDS

In these commoner puzzles, every word in both columns is the same length—but what do the words in Column A share that the words in Column B lack?

(The "Match Wits with Mensa" panel managed to answer only 30 percent of these commoners.)

1

COLUMN A	COLUMN B
Elite	Earth
Tempt	Tutor
Civic	Puppy
Label	Style
Hatch	Melts

2

COLUMN A	COLUMN B
Banana	Babble
Needed	Chimes
Horror	Tatter
Inning	Sorrow
Pepper	Murmur

3

COLUMN A	COLUMN B
Men	Fly
Ban	Son
Ice	The
War	Map
See	Oar

4

COLUMN A	COLUMN B
Pea	Wee
Why	Say
Cue	Toy
Sea	New
Owe	Cow

5

COLUMN A	COLUMN B
Bold	Flaw
Able	Gulf
Warm	They
Cold	Hike
Full	When

6

COLUMN A	COLUMN B
Emit	Lamp
Garb	Idea
Loop	Cool
Trap	Grow
Draw	Them

7

COLUMN A	COLUMN B
Cute	Fool
Side	Wide
Wash	Bond
Mass	Clap
Corn	Stun

8

COLUMN A	COLUMN B
Are	Act
Lay	Big
Hop	Urn
One	Leg
Ape	Sew

9

COLUMN A	COLUMN B
Gavel	Label
Petty	Blown
Diver	Pesky
Fight	Alone
Towel	Magic

10

COLUMN A	COLUMN B
Arch	Page
Care	Itch
Peal	Very
Many	Star
Kite	Brim

11

COLUMN A	COLUMN B
Hot	Era
Air	Get
Dip	Toy
Pry	Red
For	Arm

12

COLUMN A	COLUMN B
Proven	Gather
Loathe	Quiver
Stripe	Misery
Sacred	Octave
Fringe	Rounds

13

COLUMN A	COLUMN B
Cape	Claw
Chew	Curb
Crow	Fold
Teem	Used
Says	Mild

14

COLUMN A	COLUMN B
Flue	Mole
Flea	Feel
Coat	Evil
Crud	Sort
Flap	Nose

15

COLUMN A	COLUMN B
Real	Gold
Hare	Blue
Char	Port
Spas	Idol
Mode	Cats

NAMES AND PLACES

These commoner puzzles use the names of specific people, places, brands, and breeds. As you look for what the things in Column A share, look not just at spelling and pronunciation but also at the specifics of those people, places, brands, and breeds.

(The Mensa puzzle testers pulled in an average score of 40 percent on this section.)

1

COLUMN A
Empire State Building
Baseball Hall of Fame
Central Park
Niagara Falls
Statue of Liberty

COLUMN B
Disneyland
White House
Everglades
Alamo
Yellowstone Park

2

COLUMN A
Mercedes-Benz
Volvo
Renault
Volkswagen
Rolls-Royce

COLUMN B
Chevrolet
Toyota
Hyundai
Plymouth
Subaru

3

COLUMN A	COLUMN B
German shepherd	Greyhound
Golden retriever	Bloodhound
Norwegian elkhound	Chihuahua
Toy poodle	Husky
Irish setter	Pug

4

COLUMN A	COLUMN B
The Beatles	The Supremes
The Monkees	The Rolling Stones
The Shirelles	The Beach Boys
Creedence Clearwater Revival	The Platters
The Doors	Peter, Paul, and Mary

5

COLUMN A	COLUMN B
"Some Enchanted Evening"	"If Ever I Would Leave You"
"Oklahoma"	"Hey There"
"Do-Re-Mi"	"Maria"
"If I Loved You"	"What I Did for Love"
"Shall We Dance"	"Old Man River"

6

COLUMN A
"I Walk the Line"
"Rocky Mountain
    High"
"Imagine"
"Chances Are"
"Battle of New
    Orleans"

COLUMN B
"Strangers in the Night"
"I Left My Heart in San
    Francisco"
"The Twist"
"Love Me Tender"
"The Gambler"

7

COLUMN A
Swedish
Hebrew
Japanese
Tagalog
Hungarian

COLUMN B
French
Arabic
Portuguese
English
Spanish

8

COLUMN A
"Que Sera Sera"
"I'm Sorry"
"Walk on By"
"People"
"Where the Boys Are"

COLUMN B
"Johnny B. Goode"
"Diana"
"Blue Velvet"
"Welcome to My
    World"
"Mona Lisa"

9

COLUMN A	COLUMN B
Cubs	Twins
Red Sox	Panthers
Red Wings	Patriots
Trail Blazers	Jazz
Cowboys	Pacers

10

COLUMN A	COLUMN B
Taylor	Truman
Wilson	Lincoln
Nixon	Adams
Taft	Monroe
Pierce	Eisenhower

11

COLUMN A	COLUMN B
Columbia	Yale
Princeton	Stanford
Syracuse	Harvard
Brown	Michigan State
Duke	Southern Methodist

12

COLUMN A	COLUMN B
Vertigo	*Splendor in the Grass*
Flower Drum Song	*Gone with the Wind*
Dirty Harry	*Marty*
Bullitt	*Alfie*
The Woman in Red	*Down and Out in Beverly Hills*

13

COLUMN A	COLUMN B
Breakfast at Tiffany's	*Dirty Harry*
The Joker Is Wild	*The Odd Couple*
The Sandpiper	*Ghandi*
The Lion King	*A Streetcar Named Desire*
High Noon	*From Russia with Love*

14

COLUMN A	COLUMN B
Alexander Hamilton	John Adams
George Washington	John C. Calhoun
Andrew Jackson	Theodore Roosevelt
John F. Kennedy	Earl Warren
Franklin D. Roosevelt	John Hancock

15

COLUMN A	COLUMN B
Brazil	Canada
Switzerland	Mexico
Zaire	Iraq
Mozambique	Portugal
Belize	Japan

CIRCLE WORDS

A circle word is one that comes back around to where it started, ending with the same letter that it began with. A common circle word is *that*. As another example, how about *example?*

Circle words can be written in a circle, with the first and last letter sharing one space. That's how the puzzles in this section are laid out. For each you will see a single letter that begins and ends the answer, with blanks equal to the number of letters you have to fill in. Thus if you see the letter *s* and seven blanks, you know you're looking for a nine-letter word that starts and ends with *s*, such as *seventies*.

(The Mensa puzzle testers scored 40 percent on these circle words. For all but the last, the group came up with at least two answers.)

1

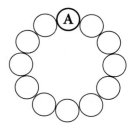

2

3

4

5

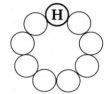

6

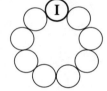

7

8

9

10

11

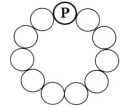

12

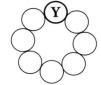

chapter

3

Jargon

Jargon is specialized vocabulary used in a particular profession, whether it's bee-keeping or bookkeeping. A punster might find a clever way to use jargon in a sentence, but puzzle solvers do things the hard way: they start with the incomplete sentence and try to figure out a word or name from the particular jargon that completes the sentence in a meaningful way.

Here are some examples using jargon from the world of art:

1. Can a man's _____ much about his future?
Solution: pastel (past tell)

2. The salesman was asked to _____ the neighborhood.
Solution: canvas

3. My father watched _____ the boat ashore.
Solution: Miro (me row)

4. The defense attorney said that a mobster tried to _____ his client.
Solution: frame ("Erase" could also work, but not "rub out," because that's two words.)

As you see, the solutions both are a single word or name from the given field *and* create a sensible sentence (grammatical, but taking some stylistic liberties). In solving these puzzles it sometimes helps to say the jargon word quickly. For an answer to be correct, it must avoid mispronunciations such as "model" for "muddle" or "sienna" for "seen a," for instance.

In each jargon category that follows, complete the sentence with an appropriate word. Then you can show your best *palette* is *hue* who is master of jargon.

MATH

The sentence "I can't believe I _____ the whole thing" can be completed with a word from the world of mathematics: *eight*. The sentence "Noah built an _____" can be completed with another bit of math jargon: *arc*. The sentence "Did Attilla the _____ the cold weather?" can be completed with *hundred*.

Find the right math jargon to make these sentences *add* up.

(The "Match Wits with Mensa" panel scored 75 percent on these questions.)

1 He came to the beach a pale man, but went home as a _____.

2 Even in good weather, a trouble-free crossing of the North _____ be guaranteed.

3 They had a handsome kitten and _____ puppy.

4 She turned down the _____ on the radio.

5 The horse placed, but never _____.

6 Because he had little credit, his parents had to _____ his car loan.

7 The most difficult part about being a good judge is deciding if sworn testimony is _____ fiction.

8 Doctor grandma always told us that good nutrition comes from eating three _____ meals each day.

9 Inflexible people have a _____ way of doing things.

10 The _____ an enemy carrier and torpedoed it.

L A W

The sentence "I'll pick a _____ there's enough cotton" can be completed with a legal term: *bailiff*. The sentence "As he got older, Beethoven's _____ got progressively worse" can be completed with *hearing*. The sentence "Ghengis _____ down many enemies" can be completed with *contract*.

Use your *judgment* to complete the following *sentences*.

(The puzzle testers from Mensa were able to find correct answers 55 percent of the time.)

1 Every citrus fruit has _____.

2 The witness with the Cockney accent said, "When 'e made _____ 'it the other bloke's motorcar."

3 There is copper _____ coin.

4 At the Celtics game, the fans kept yelling "_____!"

5 You _____ me with those chocolates, but you can't make me eat them.

6 She enjoyed a Viennese _____ with her coffee.

7 The best speeches are _____.

8 A _____ of beer usually costs a little less than four six-packs.

9 If the owners and the players'll stop bashing each other, the commissioner of the _____ try to get the parties to settle their differences.

10 After he uses a _____ for six months, the orthodontic work will be completed.

BUSINESS

The sentence "Dracula was _____" can be completed with business term: *account*. The sentence "She had a complete set of James _____ movies" can be completed with *bond*. The sentence "Once you cover your head with your red baseball _____ mean that you're part of the team" can be completed with *capital*.

See how many business jargon solutions you can *manufacture*.

(The Mensa volunteers scored 55 percent in this section.)

1 He tried to move a heavy sofa, but he couldn't _____.

2 The captain of the _____ to sail at 5:00 A.M., but he overslept.

3 Elijah was her favorite _____.

4 Take all the Frito _____ the top shelf and put it on the bottom.

5 After checking the progress of my healing broken arm, the doctor made an appointment _____ removal in two weeks.

6 The world traveler needs to know if tipping is a _____ not.

7 These _____ were designed to stand up to ninety-knot gusts of wind.

8 If you don't get a _____ means the most you can bowl is 90.

9 You can't _____ and uncles for the misdeeds of their nieces and nephews.

10 She loved old horror movies starring actors like Lugosi, Cushing, and _____.

CHEMISTRY

The sentence "I hope the carpenter will _____ this nail into the wall" can be completed with a word from the language of chemistry: *compound*. The sentence "The wrestler had one _____ the mat" can be completed with that elementary word *neon*. The sentence "On *I Love Lucy*, the Ricardos' neighbors were Fred and _____ Mertz" can be completed with *ethyl*.

Keep your *ion* these puzzles in chemistry jargon as they stir up in your brain.

(Our Mensa members completed 45 percent of these sentences correctly on average.)

1 The days of the past _____ forever.

2 The horse _____ until the final furlong.

3 The rancher compiled a _____.

4 Why has the _____ in the repair shop for three days?

5 The English restaurant had roasted _____ the menu.

6 At a Stephen King movie, when ya hear _____ scream.

7 In this parking garage, you're only charged the _____ if you enter after 6:00 P.M.

8 _____ Williams was a great swimmer.

9 The fighter said, "Let me _____."

10 Although they were unsuccessful with Gerry in 1976, the Republicans were able to _____ in 1980.

MEDICINE

The sentence "My high _____ his low diamond" can be completed with a word from medical jargon: *heartbeat*. The sentence "You can't _____ if you're over ten" can be completed with *benign*. And "The robins all _____ south for the winter," can be completed with *flu*.

Find a word in medical jargon to complete each of these *prescribed* sentences.

(At these medical mind benders the Mensa members' median measured 50 percent.)

1 If you get dandruff, your _____ itch.

2 Carly sang, "You're So _____."

3 One would find _____ a list of fuels.

4 He packed a _____ toothbrush, and a shaver.

5 When Angela asked him for something sweet, he gave _____ cracker.

6 He was great in thinkin' up new gizmos, but poor _____ 'em to see if they really worked.

7 When I was a _____ bends and sit-ups were much easier to do.

8 How _____ Lancelot be as important a part as King Arthur?

9 The tackle was _____ forward as the half-back was runnin' to his right.

10 Seeing little Suzy with an after-dinner _____ she had eaten all her vegetables.

MUSIC

The sentence "The toothpaste factory donated a _____ day to a local charity" can be completed with a word from the vocabulary of music: *tuba*. The sentence "The gift box had a _____ on it" can be completed with *bow*. The sentence "The frying pan had a wooden _____" can be completed with the name of the composer *Handel*.

Find a word or a name in musical jargon to *conduct* these sentences to their completion.

(The "Match Wits with Mensa" panel scored 55 percent on these puzzles.)

1 Mr. Capone's prison guards tried to make Big _____ the line.

2 Thy castles art filthy and thy _____ slimy.

3 If an individual _____ corporation, the names of the directors must be found.

4 _____ make it too dangerous for truckers to drive through the canyon?

5 If Nurse Barton were living today, chances are a business agent would be helping _____ substantial income for her hospital foundation.

6 Mrs. Long wrote her will _____ penny of her fortune would go into the wrong hands.

7 The children were trying to _____ the closet.

8 The sheriff looked at the ruffians, spat, and drawled, "Git feathers and _____."

9 She bought a _____ of wood.

10 In shuffleboard, a _____ an eight is a good score.

GEOGRAPHY

Countries may not share common languages, but they do make up a common jargon we can use in puzzles. The sentence "When I play Scrabble, _____ up as many points as possible" can be completed with the name of a country: *Iraq*. The sentence, "When a chanteuse is paid to _____ performance is unacceptable" can be completed with *Singapore*. And "First I walked, then I jogged, then _____" can be completed with *Iran*.

You'll ooh and ah and get one credit *Peru* as you correctly complete each of the following sentences with the name of a country.

(The Mensa puzzle testers answered 65 percent of these puzzles correctly.)

1 When he walked into his _____ Spitz could see all his swimming medals.

2 Never _____ friend into making a quick decision.

3 Though some people can't, others _____ column of numbers very quickly.

4 If you _____ number that ends in 3, the result ends in 7.

5 Pants should never be excessively tight _____ too loose.

6 Verification means making sure a statement _____.

7 When it comes to great Cardinal hitters, many think that the leader of the _____ Musial.

8 John and Olivia starred in _____.

9 The head plotter whispered, "Before you begin the _____ for my signal."

10 Her favorite jazz musician was Chick _____.

ZOOLOGY

An animal can make sense of this sentence: "The waiter gave the _____ bag and a cup of boiling water." That animal is a *manatee*. Similarly, the sentence "If Johann Sebastian were arrested, one of his sons would have paid the bail to _____ from jail" can be completed with *springbok*. And "There's a big fine to pay if your car's _____ away" can be completed with *toad*.

Bear down and unleash an animal into each of the following sentences to create a sentence that can stand on its own four legs.

(The "Match Wits with Mensa" puzzle testers soared to a 60 percent score on these jargon puzzles.)

1 The patient would often rant and _____ his padded cell.

2 Some automobile engineers think that a well-designed overhead _____ provide more horsepower.

3 The accused holdup man said he had to _____ order to eat.

4 The candidate's voice became _____ after the sixth speech.

5 It's easier to _____ guitar than a piano.

6 Her favorite song was "Let It _____."

7 Her parents watched her uncle and _____ and get married in Las Vegas.

8 Riviera, Torrey Pines, and Pebble Beach are among the best _____ on the West Coast.

9 When playing chemin de _____ is good to be dealt a four and a five.

10 Ike told Dick, "Be careful or _____ win the election."

POLITICS

For a field that relies on communication to the public, politics has developed a substantial jargon all its own. The sentence "It would take fifty kids to _____ Brown shoe store" can be completed with a term from that jargon: *filibuster*. The sentence "They found the weakest _____ the chain" can be completed with a highly regarded name in politics: *Lincoln*. The sentence "Would you prefer a Dirt Devil, a _____, or a Eureka?" can be completed with another presidential name: *Hoover*.

Elect a word or a name in American political jargon to complete these fine, upstanding sentences.

(Our Mensa members scored 65 percent on this quiz.)

1 If you invite more guests, you'll have to _____ glasses with champagne.

2 When I went to summer _____ Rand's book *The Fountainhead* was popular.

3 If you lie 20 percent of the time, you're _____ times out of ten.

4 He used an old razor and got several _____ his face.

5 Did Rock Hudson ever help Sandra _____ a hook?

6 If tomorrow is a hot day, she _____ herself at the beach.

7 When you return a _____ sure not to hit it into the net.

8 Barbie gave _____ in individuality and an A in popularity.

9 If Muppets had a senior _____ Piggy would go with Kermit.

10 Is that a tall _____ the truth?

CLOTHING

Clothes don't really make the person, but the right words from garment jargon make these sentences complete. For instance, "We _____ a circle around the campfire" can be completed with the word *satin.* The sentence "He enjoyed _____ and Vietnamese food" can be completed with another word from the jargon of garments: *tie.* And "If a ship flies the Union _____ means that it's English" can be completed with *jacket.*

Outfit the following sentences with the right word from the rag trade.

(The "Match Wits with Mensa" panel of puzzlers racked up 65 percent on these problems.)

1 It's difficult to _____ large car in a small space.

2 There were two small beds and a _____ the cabin.

3 If you want to make a traditional baseball _____ is not the wood to use.

4 The lead male role in *The Prince of Tides* went _____ Nolte.

5 They used to listen to Bob and _____ the radio.

6 It's annoying to find a cigarette _____ a no-smoking area.

7 The retired catcher kept his first _____ his den.

8 Would the ability to make a two-foot-high _____ the coach as the minimum standard for making the basketball team?

9 If Steve Martin made a detergent commercial for _____ Moranis could be a pitchman for Tide.

10 Pennsylvania is known for its _____ fly pie.

WHAT'S NEXT?

You can challenge your math skills with number sequences such as, "1, 4, 9, 16, 25, ___." (The next number is 36, the next perfect square.) But this is an A-B-C quiz book, so we have *non-number* sequences to challenge your other thinking skills. For example:

O, T, T, F, F, S, S, E, ___
Solution: N (This sequence is made up of the first letters in "one, two, three, . . . ")

fly, spider, bird, cat, dog, _____
Solution: horse (This is the next thing the "old lady" swallowed in the children's song.)

Johnson, Humphrey, Agnew, Ford, Rockefeller, Mondale, _____
Solution: Bush (This is a sequence of U.S. vice presidents since Lyndon Johnson.)

Complete these "What's Next?" puzzles by identifying the next item in the sequence, stating the underlying reasoning, or both.

(Our panel of Mensa puzzle testers scored 50 percent on this section.)

1 Hillary, Barbara, Nancy, Rosalynn, Betty, Patricia, _____

2 M, V, E, M, J, S, U, N, _____

3 H, He, Li, Be, B, C, _____

4 Kefauver, Lodge, Miller, Muskie, Shriver, _____

5 A, K, Q, J, _____

6 Argentina, Bolivia, Brazil, Chile, Colombia, _____

7 Skies, grain, majesties, _____

8 Deer, drop, name, long, needle, note, _____

9 Athens, Paris, St. Louis, Athens, London, Stockholm, Antwerp, Paris, Amsterdam, Los Angeles, _____

10 Infant, toddler, child, adolescent, _____

11 Calgary, Vancouver, Winnipeg, Saint John, St. John's, Yellowknife, _____

12 Badgers, Boilermakers, Buckeyes, Fighting Illini, Gophers, _____

13 A, T, G, C, L, V, L, S, S, C, A, _____

14 Patterson, Johannsen, Patterson, Liston, _____

15 George, Ronald, Gerald, Richard, Dwight, _____

chapter 4

Pencil-Optional Puzzles

MISSING-LETTER SCRAMBLES

Anagrams are one of the oldest and most popular forms of word games. They involve mixing the letters of a word up to spell a new word, as in turning *names* into *Mensa,* or unscrambling a group of letters into a word. Missing-letter scrambles take anagrams one step further by removing two or more of the mixed-up letters and then challenging you to solve them. For example, to each of the following groups of letters restore just two letters to make an anagram from which to form a word.

H P Y Z

Solution: Add *e* and *r* to make the makings of *zephyr.*

B J N

Solution: Add *o* and *a* and unscramble *banjo*.

For each puzzle below, identify the *two* missing letters and then unscramble all the letters to form a word.

(The "Match Wits with Mensa" panel answered 60 percent of these puzzles accurately.)

1   U U V

2   J R R U Y

3   N Q U U

4   A B C U V

5   R T U Z

6   **A A A T T**

7   **F M M O U**

8   **N N N O U**

9   **A L U U U**

10   **D F J**

11   **A B I R W**

12   **A K Q T U**

13   **B Q R U U**

These last two puzzles each have *three* missing letters. Find them and unscramble the letters to form a word.

14   **G K K L U**

15   **A I I I N N**

LETTER SEQUENCES

Some common words contain uncommon letter sequences. For example, *vodka* has the sequence *dka*. As another example, *skiing* has the sequence *kiin*.

Try to fill out the English words that contain the listed sequence of consecutive letters.

(Our puzzle testers from Mensa successfully identified 50 percent of the words, on average.)

1   **XYG**

2   **OPSOI**

3   **UPTC**

4   **NKYA**

5   **URTSH**

6   **AKFA**

7   **NNERM**

8   **RDAMO**

9   **UEBI**

10   **NDTHR**

11   **EZVO**

12   **ALFUN**

13   **SQUERA**

14   **AELST**

15   **XSW**

VANITY TELEPHONE NUMBERS

On a standard late-twentieth century telephone, the buttons are set up like this:

1	**2** **ABC**	**3** **DEF**
4 **GHI**	**5** **JKL**	**6** **MNO**
7 **PRS**	**8** **TUV**	**9** **WXY**
*	**0**	**#**

Some people and businesses use vanity telephone numbers, which can be dialed using letters related to what that person or business does. For example, a dog trainer may want 748-7829, which can be reached by dialing "SIT-STAY." A bodybuilding gymnasium may want 466-3227, which can be reached by dialing "GOOD-ABS."

What word or words would each of these people or businesses give out as a vanity telephone number?

(This section may have increased the vanity of our Mensa panel as they averaged 85 percent on these puzzles.)

1
A deli at **742-5537**

2
An attorney at **529-7848**

3
A butcher shop at **747-5646**

4
A classical music radio station at **332-8779**

5
A private detective agency at **486-7463**

6
A pizzeria at **262-4689**

7
A tavern at **268-7266**

8
A consumer advocacy group at **729-3325**

9
A cheese company at **243-3327**

10
A farmer at **427-8378**

11

A French language school at **266-5687**

12

A credit card company at **752-7842**

13

A poison control hotline at **277-3642**

14

A sports announcer at **465-9269**

15

Funk & Wagnalls at **539-4266**

WORD MAKERS

This is one of the simplest forms of word puzzles, found in many puzzle books for young children:

> How many new words can you make from the letters in Mensa?
>
> *Solution:* Names, means, amens, seam, same, sane, mane, mesa, mean, men, man, . . .

The puzzles in this section follow the same pattern, except that your goal is to create a word of a certain length—a fairly long length, at that—from the letters of a famous movie title.

For instance, *The Last Picture Show* contains one *a*, one *c*, two *e*s, two *h*s, one *i*, one *l*, one *o*, one *p*, one *r*, two *s*s, three *t*s, one *u*, and one *w*. From that assortment one can form the twelve-letter word *therapeutics*.

For each of the following movie titles, form at least one word of the specified length.

(Between them the "Match Wits with Mensa" testers managed to find at least two words of sufficient length for each of these movie titles, except for the last. Individually, however, they averaged just 30 percent on this section.)

1

An eleven-letter word in
From Russia with Love

2

A seven-letter word in
On the Beach

3

A twelve-letter word in
Down and Out in Beverly Hills

4

A ten-letter word in
Raiders of the Lost Ark

5

An eight-letter word in
Lilies of the Field

6

A nine-letter word in
You Only Live Twice

7

An eleven-letter word in
James and the Giant Peach

8

An eleven-letter word in
The Philadelphia Story

9

An eight-letter word in
A Fish Called Wanda

10

A seven-letter word in
Cape Fear

chapter
5

Grab Bag

Now that you've learned how to do all the puzzles in this book, it's time to do them all again.

1 Who am I?

In rush-hour traffic, I claim,
The signature of my last name
Appears in large size
To the road-weary eyes—
Of the thousands who say I'm to blame.

Identify the following movie titles:

2

DEPRIVED OF DREAMS WHILE OVERLOOKING PUGET SOUND

3

THE MANNER IN WHICH YOU AND I HERETOFORE EXISTED

4

Abraham Jefferson Roosevelt Polk, the Hollywood producer, loved American holidays. To get into the proper mood, he had a habit of spending the evening before each holiday listening to an appropriate speech from history. He listened to a reading of the Declaration of Independence on the evening before July 4. He listened to a recital of the Gettysburg Address before Presidents' Day. One evening in 1994, Polk listened to one such speech and went to bed. Early the next morning, through no fault of his own or anyone else's, Polk found his CD player was badly damaged. Whose speeches had Polk played the night before?

Identify the following series of abbreviations:

5

VANF, NEAP, ROCR, CHEV, CHOC, TINR

6

EUC, FIC, MAP, RED, SEQ, JAC, POP, MAG

7

Identify the real title of this florid song (also the title of a movie):

A trio of metallic tender located in the generator of continuous parabolic bursts of water

8

Invent a threeesque that means
RIGHT OUT OF THE DRYER

Commoner puzzles: What do the words in the first column share that the words in the second column do not?

9

COLUMN A	COLUMN B
Football	Tennis
Basketball	Volleyball
Hockey	Baseball
Lacrosse	Bowling
Soccer	Golf

10

COLUMN A	COLUMN B
Mail	Plan
Pairs	Grapes
Quoit	Pledge
Louse	Party
More	Exit

11

COLUMN A	COLUMN B
Grove	Part
Date	North
Handle	Pile
Age	Dairy
Or	Item

12

COLUMN A	COLUMN B
Thirsty	Hungry
Unopposed	Force
Defined	Yacht
Weighing	Impolite
Student	Outlasted

13

COLUMN A	COLUMN B
Grouch	Bag
Page	Gift
Graft	Fang
Zing	Brought
Gone	Gnaw

14

COLUMN A	COLUMN B
New York	Phoenix
City	Miami
Cincinnati	Atlantic City
St. Louis	Los Angeles
Philadelphia	Denver
Memphis	

15

Complete this sentence with a term from chemistry jargon:

When an athlete turns _____ becomes part of the job.

16

Complete this sentence with the name of a country:

She used to stand at the piano and sing "_____ Malone."

17

Complete this sentence using a word from zoology:

> For the armorer to make a powerful _____ long, strong piece of wood must be cut and prepared.

18

Complete this sentence with a term from clothing jargon:

> When we entered the pub, we saw many old _____ at the bar.

19

What comes next in this sequence?

P, N, B, R, ____

20

What comes next in this sequence?

E, A, D, G, B, ____

21

Add two letters to the following assortment and arrange all the letters into a new word:

A A C C U

22

Add *three* letters to the following assortment and arrange all the letters into a new word:

M T Y Y

23

Add three letters to the following assortment and arrange them into a new word:

H H Y

Identify the standard English words that contain the following letter sequences (with no hyphens between the letters):

24
ALDEH

25
VERSM

26
CKSK

27
ANHO

28

Anita Lo, D.D.S., obtained this vanity phone number:

345-5464

What word or phrase does Dr. Lo tell her patients to dial in order to make an appointment?

29

Form an eight- or, better yet, a nine-letter word
from the letters of this movie:

Some Like It Hot

Solutions

The percentages in parentheses are the "Match Wits with Mensa" results for individual puzzles.

CHAPTER 1: NO-PENCIL QUICKIES

LIMERICKS

1. Gravity (90%)

2. The unknown soldier (65%)

3. Hydrogen (85%)

4. The past (40%)

5. Calorie (65%)

6. Detroit (70%). Windsor, Ontario, is immediately south of downtown Detroit.

7. i (55%). i is the mathematical symbol for the square root of -1.

8. A translator or interpreter (55%)

9. Mark (55%)

FLOWERY MOVIE TITLES

1. *Hello, Dolly* (85%)

2. *Raging Bull* (60%)

3. *West Side Story* (55%)

4. *The Big Easy* (80%)

5. *Planet of the Apes* (60%)

6. *Speed* (70%)

7. *Gone with the Wind* (60%)

8. *Leaving Las Vegas* (85%)

STRANGE QUESTIONS

1. The 5s and the 10s (75%). A straight flush requires five consecutive cards of the same suit. Removing the 5s and 10s will allow consecutive card sequences of A–K–Q–J, 9–8–7–6, or 4–3–2–A only. This eliminates all possible straights and straight flushes.

2. 50 (50%). The word *mean* signifies the average of a group of numbers. Therefore, the missing number—along with 30, 35, 45, and 40—must average 40. This can be solved using algebra or

more quickly with the "over and under" method. Thirty is 10 under the average and 35 is 5 under the average, so the "unders" are 15 below the average. 45 is 5 over the average and the "overs" need to be 15 above the average to make up for the "unders." So the missing number has to be 10 over the average, or 50.

3. Dr. Masterson was watching or perhaps even performing in *The Music Man* (50%). "Gary, Indiana" is a song from that show by Meredith Wilson. Dr. Masterson could also have been operating on a patient named Gary Indiana somewhere else in the hospital.

4. Kucic was oversensitive to booing fans (65%). In the telephone conversation, the words *boos* and *booze* were indistinguishable.

5. Santiago played softly (70%). The musical term *piano* means "low in volume." The original word for the large musical instrument with black-and-white keys was *pianoforte* because it could be played softly or loudly.

6. The Tampa Bay Buccaneers (30%). There are numerous "bay areas," but only two have NFL football teams: San Francisco/Oakland and Tampa Bay. Driving 120 miles east of San Francisco would get you to Sacramento, but driving 120 miles east of Tampa would get you to the Atlantic Ocean. The 49ers were the visiting team.

7. Jack (55%). Pilots get upset when they hear *hijack* or *hijacking*.

8. Aluminum (40%). In England this element is spelled "aluminium" and pronounced with the accent on the third syllable. Not sulfur vs. sulphur. Both these spellings are used by Americans.

9. Golf course (95%). In golf, "shooting an eagle" means scoring two under par.

10. Postage stamps (30%). In 1997, first-class postage stamps were 32 cents each, and buying twelve stamps from a standard stamp machine with a five-dollar bill would bring back four coins: a Susan B. Anthony dollar, a dime, a nickel, and a penny.

ABBREVIATIONS

1. Mathematics courses: arithmetic, algebra, geometry, trigonometry, probability, statistics, calculus (90%).

2. Movie/video types: comedy, drama, adventure, action, sports, musicals, horror, science fiction (80%).

3. Orchestral instruments: violin, viola, cello, bass, trumpet, trombone, french horn (60%).

4. Television/electronics brand names: Sony,

Samsung, Mitsubishi, Goldstar, Toshiba, Panasonic, Zenith, Quasar (20%).

5. NBA basketball teams: Celtics, Knicks, Bulls, Rockets, Cavaliers, Jazz, Lakers (80%).

6. U.S. airports: New York–La Guardia Airport, Los Angeles International Airport, San Francisco International Airport, Dallas–Love Field, Seattle–Tacoma Airport, Miami International Airport, Detroit Municipal Airport (80%).

7. U.S. national parks: Yosemite, Yellowstone, Olympia, Glacier, Carlsbad Caverns, Mammoth Caves, Everglades, Shenandoah (80%).

8. Tire brand names: Firestone, Goodyear, Dunlop, Goodrich, Michelin, Kelly, Uniroyal (25%).

FLOWERY SONG TITLES

1. "Raindrops Keep Fallin' on My Head" from *Butch Cassidy and the Sundance Kid* (95%)

2. "High Hopes" from *A Hole in the Head* (90%)

3. "When You Wish upon a Star" from *Pinocchio* (50%)

4. "As Time Goes By" from *Casablanca* (40%)

5. "Someday My Prince Will Come" from *Snow White and the Seven Dwarfs* (75%)

6. "Whistle While You Work" from *Snow White and the Seven Dwarfs* (85%)

7. "Over the Rainbow" from *The Wizard of Oz* (80%)

8. "Let's Go Fly a Kite" from *Mary Poppins* (45%)

9. "Candy Man" from *Willie Wonka and the Chocolate Factory* (40%)

10. "Everybody's Talkin' " from *Midnight Cowboy* (45%)

THREEESQUES

1. Halllord, halllessor, halllandlord, and hallleaser (65%). If a person who owns land is a land-lord, one who owns a hall would be a *halllord.*

2. Egggraph, egggram, and egggauge (75%). If a chart of pictures is a pictograph, a chart of egg production would be an *egggraph.*

3. Grimmmaster, Grimmmaven, Grimmman, and faultlessstoryteller (40%). If a chess expert can be a chessmaster, a fairy-tale expert would be a *Grimmmaster.*

4. Daleeer, hilllover, knolllover, knollloper, bluff-fanatic, foothilllover, hillloper, knollleaper, and knolllegger (25%). If a serious mountain climber is a mountaineer, a climber of dales would be a *daleeer.*

5. Kangarooology, Rooology, and Kangarooobser-vations (70%). If the study of society is sociol-ogy, the study of kangaroos would be *kanga-rooology.*

6. Errroom, errregion, errrealm, errrange, errrink, and missspot (55%). If a place to dance is a ballroom, a place to err would be an *errroom.*

7. Watttime, watttenure, wattterm, and stilllit (50%). If the amount of time that something is not in use is downtime, the amount of time

that a bulb's watttage is in use would be *watt-time.*

8. Odddial, or odddetector (45%). If a fellow who is odd may be an Oddfellow, a dial that is odd could be an *odddial.*

CHAPTER 2: COMMONER PUZZLES

MISCELLANY

1. All the things in Column A contain water (65%). They are not simply mixtures (steel in Column B is an alloy of different metals).

2. All the fruits listed in Column A end in *e*. (65%).

3. All the words in Column A can be used before or after the word *iron:* iron lung, cast iron, iron horse, iron maiden, and gridiron (70%).

4. All the items listed in Column A are gifts mentioned in "The Twelve Days of Christmas" (75%).

5. All words listed in Column A are animal names that can also serve as common verbs (45%).

6. All the elements in Column A have chemical symbols that start with a different letter: mercury is Hg, gold is Au, iron is Fe, potassium is K, and lead is Pb (35%).

7. Each word in Column A can form a new word if *ship* is added at the end (45%).

8. All the words in Column A have exactly one of each vowel (40%).

9. All the words in Column A represent things or ways one can "bear" (25%).

10. All the animal names listed in Column A end in two vowels (30%).

11. Each word in Column A can form another word if *et* is added at the end: junket, blanket, casket, socket, and market (45%).

12. Each word in Column A can form a new word if *ment* is added at the end: figment, casement, easement, pigment, and basement (30%).

13. All the words listed in Column A have a *k* sound (30%).

14. Each word in Column A can form a new word if *g* is added at the beginning: gastro-nomical, graze, gape, gloom, and glistening (30%).

15. Each word in Column A can form a new word or common expression by preceding it with the word *hard:* hard facts, hard-boiled, hardware, hard knocks, and hard pressed (40%).

SAME-SIZE WORDS

1. All the five-letter words in Column A begin and end with the same letter (65%).

2. All the six-letter words in Column A have three of one letter *and* two of another (30%).

3. Each three-letter word in Column A can form another word with *d* added at the end: mend, bend, iced, ward, and seed (25%).

4. The three-letter words in Column A are homonyms of a letter of the alphabet: P, Y, Q, C, and O (55%).

5. The four-letter words in Column A are adjectives (30%).

6. Each of the four-letter words in Column A can form another word if its letters are reversed: time, brag, pool, part, and ward (30%).

7. Each of the four-letter words in Column A can form a new word if *a* is added at the beginning: acute, aside, awash, amass, and acorn (30%).

8. Each of the three-letter words in Column A can form a new word if *c* is added at the beginning: care, clay, chop, cone, and cape (40%).

9. Each of the five-letter words in Column A can form a new word if *r* is added after the first letter: gravel, pretty, driver, fright, and trowel (40%).

10. Each of the four-letter words in Column A can form a new word if you delete the last letter: arc, car, pea, man, and kit (25%).

11. The letters in all the three-letters words in Column A are in alphabetical order (10%).

12. Each of the six-letter words in Column A can form another word if the first and last letters are deleted: rove, oath, trip, acre, and ring (25%).

13. Each of the four-letter words in Column A can form another word if *es* is added at the beginning: escape, eschew, escrow, esteem, and essays (35%).

14. Each of the four-letter words in Column A can form another word if the last letter is changed to *x*: flux, flex, coax, crux, and flax (5%).

15. Each of the four-letter words in Column A can form a new word if *m* is added at the end: realm, harem, charm, spasm, and modem (35%).

NAMES AND PLACES

1. All the attractions listed in Column A are in the state of New York (95%).

2. All the cars listed in Column A are European, not simply foreign (70%).

3. The dog breeds listed in Column A consist of two words (80%).

4. At the height of their chart success, the musical groups listed in Column A had four members (25%).

5. The show songs listed in Column A were written by Rodgers and Hammerstein (30%).

6. The songs listed in Column A were originally sung by a John or a Johnny: Cash, Denver, Lennon, Mathis, and Horton (30%).

7. The languages listed in Column A are official languages of one country only (15%).

8. The songs listed in Column A were originally sung by women: Doris Day, Brenda Lee, Dionne Warwick, Barbra Streisand, and Connie Francis (40%).

9. The sports teams listed in Column A represent a specific city (Chicago, Boston, Detroit, Portland, and Dallas) as opposed to a region (Minnesota, Carolina, New England, Utah, and Indiana) (25%). Of course, pro sports being how they are, this solution is good only as of the date of publication!

10. The commonly used first name of each of the presidents listed in Column A is longer than his surname: Zachary Taylor, Woodrow Wilson, Richard Nixon, William Taft, and Franklin Pierce (5%).

11. The universities listed in Column A are in

states with two-word names: New York, New Jersey, New York, Rhode Island, and North Carolina (10%).

12. The movies listed in Column A were set primarily in San Francisco (15%).

13. The movies listed in Column A won an Academy Award for best song: "Moon River," "All the Way," "The Shadow of Your Smile," "Can You Feel the Love Tonight?" and "High Noon (Do Not Forsake Me, Oh My Darlin')" (15%).

14. The famous Americans listed in Column A have had their faces depicted on money (35%).

15. The countries listed in Column A contain the letter *z* (60%).

CIRCLE WORDS

1. Arachnophobia, anisometropia (30%)
2. Characteristic, claustrophobic, chromatophoric (55%)
3. Fisticuff, fireproof, foodstuff (40%)
4. Gerrymandering, grandfathering, groundbreaking (40%)
5. Henceforth, heliograph, hallelujah, hieroglyph, heathenish, horselaugh, hydrograph (40%)
6. Intermezzi, illuminati (25%)
7. Kickback, kinsfolk, kerplunk, knapsack (60%)
8. Moratorium, molybdenum, memorandum, mainstream, militarism, myocardium, metabolism, monarchism (50%)
9. Oratorio, ocotillo, ostinato (50%)
10. Withdraw or withdrew, williwaw, windflaw (50%)
11. Partisanship or partizanship (15%)
12. Yesterday (60%)

CHAPTER 3: JARGON

MATH

1. Tangent (80%)
2. Secant (65%)
3. Acute (70%)
4. Volume or power (90%); not hypotenuse— that's not close enough to "hyped-up news."
5. One (95%)
6. Cosine (85%)
7. Factor (70%), also part and pure
8. Square or solid (95%)
9. Set, solid, linear, and straight (60%).
10. Subtract (45%)

LAW

1. Appeal, cedes, and sections (60%)
2. Attorney (60%)
3. Innocent (35%)
4. Defense (20%)
5. Contempt, bribe, and present (70%)
6. Tort (35%)
7. Brief (50%)

8. Case (90%)

9. Legal (40%)

10. Retainer or mouthpiece (65%)

BUSINESS

1. Budget or manage (85%)

2. Shipment (55%)

3. Profit (80%)

4. Layoff (60%)

5. Forecast (85%)

6. Customer (55%)

7. Sales (60%)

8. Market (but not strike) (25%)

9. Finance (15%), not blamants or defendants (legal terms)

10. Price (35%)

CHEMISTRY

1. Argon (90%)

2. Lead (55%)

3. Catalyst, table, and volume (20%)

4. Carbon (90%)

5. Boron (40%)

6. Ammonia (10%)

7. Nitrate (20%)

8. Ester (55%)

9. Atom (60%)

10. Electron (30%)

MEDICINE

1. Scalpel (95%)

2. Vein (80%)

3. Colon (45%)

4. Coma (30%)

5. Angiogram (25%)

6. Intestine (55%)

7. Kidney (50%)

8. Cancer (80%)

9. Surgeon or tendon (15%), also blocking and cutting

10. Treatment (40%)

MUSIC

1. Alto (80%)

2. Mozart (60%)

3. Sousa (50%)

4. Woodwind or woodwinds (25%)

5. Clarinet (45%), also score

6. Sonata (65%)

7. Haydn (55%)

8. Guitar (35%)

9. Chord, staff, and Bloch (85%)

10. Tenor (40%)

GEOGRAPHY

1. Denmark (85%)

2. Russia (50%)

3. Canada (80%)

4. Cuba (35%)

5. Norway (50%)

6. Israel (65%)

7. Pakistan (80%)

8. Greece (75%)

9. Kuwait (70%)

10. Korea (50%)

ZOOLOGY

1. Raven (90%), also lion (but just *"bearly"*)
2. Camel (60%)
3. Robin (75%), not lion
4. Horse or husky (90%)
5. Tuna (50%), also paca
6. Bee (85%)
7. Antelope (45%), not ant
8. Lynx (30%)
9. Ferret (55%)
10. Jackal (35%), not eel

POLITICS

1. Fillmore (80%)
2. Campaign (70%), not Camp David
3. Candidate (10%)
4. Nixon (90%)
5. Debate (55%)
6. Wilson (70%)
7. Lobby (30%)
8. Kennedy (75%)
9. Promise (75%)
10. Taylor (90%)

CLOTHING

1. Parka (90%)
2. Cotton (65%)
3. Batik (40%)
4. Tunic (85%)
5. Rayon (70%)
6. Button (75%)
7. Mitten (85%)
8. Jumpsuit (30%)
9. Fabric (20%)
10. Shoe (80%)

WHAT'S NEXT?

1. Lady Bird (65%). This is a sequence of first names of first ladies, going back from Hillary Clinton. You get extra credit if you knew Lady Bird Johnson's real name was Claudia.

2. P (75%). This is a sequence of the first letters of the planets, and Pluto is last.

3. N (60%). This is a sequence of elements on the periodic table, and nitrogen is next.

4. Dole (15%). This is a sequence of losing vice presidential nominees, starting with Kefauver in 1956.

5. 10 or T (80%). This is a sequence of card values in poker.

6. Ecuador (65%). This is a listing of South American countries in alphabetical order.

7. Plain (80%). These are the last words in the lines of "America the Beautiful."

8. Drink (35%). This a sequence of words following the notes of the scale in Rodgers and Hammerstein's "Do-Re-Mi": "Doe, a deer... Ray, a drop... Me, a name... Far, a long... Sew, a needle... La, a note... Tea, a drink..."

9. Berlin (20%). This is a chronological sequence of cities that hosted the modern summer Olympics, starting in 1896.

10. Adult (60%). This is a sequence of growth stages.

11. Halifax (20%). To arrive at this answer, arrange the Canadian provinces alphabetically and then list the city with the largest population in each of the provinces.

12. Hawkeyes (30%). Big Ten team names in alphabetical order.

13. P (10%). These are the first letters of the astrological signs in columnist Sydney Omarr's order, and Pisces is next.

14. Ali or Clay (50%). This is a sequence of world heavyweight boxing champions.

15. Herbert (45%). This is a sequence of first names of Republican presidents, going back from Bush.

CHAPTER 4: PENCIL-OPTIONAL PUZZLES

MISSING-LETTER SCRAMBLES

1. Uvula (75%)

2. Perjury or juryrig (50%)

3. Unique (40%)

4. Bivouac (35%)

5. Quartz (25%)

6. Cantata or ratatat (30%)

7. Flummox (20%)

8. Unknown (30%)

9. Unusual (35%)

10. Fjord (40%)

11. Rainbow (15%)

12. Kumquat (25%)

13. Brusque (35%)

14. Skulking (20%)

15. Initiation or initialing (30%)

LETTER SEQUENCES

1. Oxygen (70%)

2. Topsoil (80%)

3. Bankruptcy (40%)

4. Junkyard (45%)

5. Courtship (55%)

6. Breakfast (50%)

7. Innermost (55%)

8. Cardamom (25%)

9. Bluebird (30%)

10. Spendthrift (25%)

11. Rendezvous (50%)

12. Malfunction (40%)

13. Masquerade (70%)

14. Maelstrom (65%)

15. Coxswain (30%)

VANITY TELEPHONE NUMBERS

1. Pickles (85%)

2. Lawsuit (90%)

3. Sirloin (90%)

4. Debussy (80%)

5. Gumshoe (90%)

6. Anchovy (90%)

7. Bourbon (70%)

8. Raw deal (85%)

9. Cheddar (90%)

10. Harvest (90%)

11. Bonjour (80%)

12. Plastic (90%)

13. Arsenic (85%)

14. Holy cow (75%)

15. Lexicon (85%)

WORD MAKERS

1. Formalities, formulators, isothermals, silver-smith, meritorious, liverwursts (15%)

2. Heathen, beneath, acetone, cheetah (45%)

3. Outlandishly, evolutionary, deliberation, unshovelable (25%)

4. Fortressed, fatherless, tetrahedra, rehearsals, falsehoods, terrorists (20%)

5. Filleted, hilliest, hillside (25%)

6. Violently, convolute, cotillion, evolution (30%)

7. Decapitates, emancipated, antecedents, eighteenths, detainments (15%)

8. Philatelist, diphtherial, editorially, peridotites, hospitality (25%)

9. Flinched, windfall, alliance, sandwich, swindled, hacienda, dwindles, chainsaw (35%)

10. Preface (70%)

CHAPTER 5: GRAB BAG

1. Henry Ford, who popularized the automobile in America and whose signature is the logo on millions of Ford vehicles (25%)

2. *Sleepless in Seattle* (95%)

3. *The Way We Were* (95%)

4. Polk had played a recording of Martin Luther King Jr. Early on Martin Luther King Day in 1994 there was a powerful earthquake in southern California, which damaged Polk's CD player. (20%)

5. Flavors of ice cream: vanilla fudge, Neapolitan, rocky road, cherry vanilla, chocolate, tin roof (55%)

6. Types of trees: eucalyptus, ficus, maple, redwood, sequoia, jacaranda, poplar, magnolia (50%)

7. *Three Coins in the Fountain* (90%)

8. If being filled with care is careful, then being filled with fluff from the dryer could be *fluffful* (25%).

9. The sports in Column A are all timed games in which players can score goals (25%).

10. All the words in Column A are anagrams of world capitals: Lima, Paris, Quito, Seoul, and Rome (10%).

11. If you add *man* before all the words in Column A, they form new words: mangrove, mandate, manhandle, manage, manor (20%).

12. In each of the words in Column A there is a series of three letters as they appear in alphabetical order: *rst* in thirsty, for instance (10%).

13. All the words in Column A can form new words if their *g* is replaced by a *c:* crouch, pace, craft, zinc, cone (10%).

14. All the cities in Column A border another American state (5%).

15. Propane (10%)

16. Mali (25%)

17. Boa (5%)

18. Chaps, soles, or loafers (10%)

19. Q (5%). This sequence lists the official symbols of chess pieces in order of strength; a knight is designated as N.

20. E (15%). This is the sequence of guitar strings from lowest to highest pitch.

21. Accrual, accusal (25%)

22. Mystery, mystify, mythify (35%)

23. Highly, hyphen, rhythm (50%)

24. Formaldehyde, aldehyde (50%)

25. Silversmith (30%)

26. Buckskin (35%)

27. Manhole, manhood, womanhood (50%); not man-hour, since that requires a hyphen

28. Dr. Lo's vanity phone number is Filling (95%).

29. Eight letters: milkiest, smoothie, toilsome, homilies, homelike;
nine letters: mistletoe and homeliest (35%)

How to Join Mensa

Mensa has a triple meaning in Latin: it means "mind," "table," and "month," which suggests a monthly meeting of great minds around a table. The society was founded in Great Britain in 1946 by two barristers, Roland Berrill and Dr. Lionel Ware. American Mensa was started in 1960 at the Brooklyn home of Peter and Ines Sturgeon; there were seven members at that meeting, but within three years the roll had grown to over a thousand across North America. In 1967 Mensa Canada became a separate society. As of 1997, there are more than 45,000 members of American Mensa and 3,000 members of Mensa Canada. Worldwide more than 100,000 Mensans represent over a hundred countries.

The only qualification for membership in Mensa is a score in the top 2 percent of the general population on a standardized intelligence test. American Mensa accepts over two hundred tests for membership. It also offers a battery of culturally fair, nonlanguage intelligence tests (for applicants over the age of fourteen), supervised by a certified Mensa proctor. An applicant who scores at or above the 98th percentile in any one of these exams qualifies for membership. Here are the qualifying scores on some common tests:

COLLEGE SAT (MATH AND VERBAL COMBINED)

prior to 9/30/77	1300
10/1/77 to 1/31/94	1250
after 2/1/94	not accepted

GRE

prior to 6/30/94 (math and verbal combined)	1250
after 6/30/94 (verbal, quantitative, and analytical)	1875

CALIFORNIA TEST OF MENTAL MATURITY

IQ 132

MILLER ANALOGIES TEST

(raw score) 66

STANFORD-BINET INTELLIGENCE SCALE (ANY FORM)

IQ 132

WECHSLER ADULT INTELLIGENCE SCALE AND WECHSLER
INTELLIGENCE SCALE FOR CHILDREN (ANY FORM)

IQ 132

The onetime processing fee for submitting scores from a prior test is $20. To take a supervised Mensa admission test, the fee is $25. Mensa Canada's fees for the equivalent are $25 and $40, respectively.

After an applicant's score has been accepted, he or she is invited to join a local chapter of Mensa. There are 140 chapters of American Mensa in the fifty states, Puerto Rico, and the Virgin Islands. These groups gather at least once a month, with most meeting weekly. There are also more than 150 Special Interest Groups (SIGs) that communicate regularly through newsletters and other media. The interests run the gamut from arts and crafts through chocolate, Monty Python, and skiing to zydeco music. Each year American Mensa has a national convention hosted by one local chapter. Current dues for membership in American Mensa are $45 per year. The annual dues for Mensa Canada are $55.50.

For more information please contact

American Mensa, Ltd.
201 Main Street, Suite 1101
Fort Worth, TX 76102
(800) 66-MENSA, ext. 9710
AmericanMensa@compuserve.com
http://www.us.mensa.org

Mensa Canada
329 March Road
Suite 232, Box 11
Kanata, ON   K2K 2E1
(613) 599-5897
mensa@canadamail.com
http://www.canada.mensa.org/

International Mensa (for information on other national branches of the society)

http://www.mensa.org

The "Match Wits with Mensa" Series
published by Perseus Books

The Mensa Genius Quiz Book
Marvin Grosswirth, Dr. Abbie F. Salny, and the members of Mensa
introduction by Isaac Asimov
144 pages, 0-201-05959-2, $9.00

The Mensa Genius Quiz Book 2
Marvin Grosswirth, Dr. Abbie F. Salny, and the members of Mensa
160 pages, 0-201-05958-4, $9.00

The Mensa Genius Quiz-a-Day Book
Dr. Abbie F. Salny and the members of Mensa
192 pages, 0-201-13549-3, $10.00

Proceeds from the sale of these books help fund scholarships granted by the Mensa Education and Research Fund.